WHAT IS SOCIALISM?

NICK HUNTER

Gareth Stevens
Publishing

Please visit our website, www.garethstevens.com. For a free color catalog of all our
high-quality books, call toll free 1-800-542-2595 or fax 1-877-542-2596.

Library of Congress Cataloging-in-Publication Data

Hunter, Nick.
 What is socialism? / by Nick Hunter.
    pages cm. — (Understanding political systems)
 Includes index.
 ISBN 978-1-4824-0322-0 (pbk.)
 ISBN 978-1-4824-3305-0 (6-pack)
 ISBN 978-1-4824-0321-3 (library binding)
 1. Socialism—Juvenile literature. I. Title.
 HX73.H87 2013
 320.53'1—dc23
                                    2013028417
First Edition

Published in 2014 by
Gareth Stevens Publishing
111 East 14th Street, Suite 349
New York, NY 10003

© 2014 Gareth Stevens Publishing

Produced by Calcium, www.calciumcreative.co.uk
Designed by Keith Williams and Paul Myerscough
Edited by Sarah Eason

Photo credits: Cover: Dreamstime: Alena2909 (right), Shutterstock: Alvaro German Vilela (left). Inside:
Dreamstime: Alenmax 36, Bayda127 41, Bellafotosolo 39, Cornelius20 38, Dubesor 43, Kpikoulas 42,
Sydney 44, Tonyv3112 40, Tribalium 45, Tzooka 37; Shutterstock: 3777190317 27, Alicar 15, Andrey_Popov
28, Bikeriderlondon 16, 31, Blend Images 19, David Burrows 32, Pablo Calvog 33, Hung Chung Chih 20,
CJM Grafx 25, Gordeev20 21, Rob Kints 5, Georgios Kollidas 17, Mffoto 24, Andrey_Popov 29, Natursports
18, Neveshkin Nikolay 7, Nneirda 26, Northfoto 1, 34, Onairda 35, Nick Pavlakis 6, Jan S. 30, Tribalium 4,
Yangchao 9; Wikipedia: 14, 22, 23r, Rea Irvin, Library of Congress 23l, Dorothea Lange, U.S. Farm Security
Administration/Library of Congress 13, PD-US. 12, Soyuzfoto, Library of Congress 10, Victorgrigas 11,
William Bell Scott, Alcinoe 8.

Printed in the United States of America

CPSIA compliance information: Batch # CW14GS: For further information contact Gareth Stevens, New York, New York at 1-800-542-2595.

Contents

CHAPTER ONE: What Is Socialism?   4

CHAPTER TWO: Types of Socialism   16

CHAPTER THREE: How Socialism Works   24

CHAPTER FOUR: Living with Socialism   34

CHAPTER FIVE: A Future for Socialism?   40

GLOSSARY   46

FOR MORE INFORMATION   47

INDEX   48

What Is Socialism?

Television and the media are full of stories about fabulously rich people and the wonderful lives they lead with their huge houses, private jets, and fashionable clothes. You may have seen these stories and thought, "That's not fair. Why do they have more than me?" You might have learned about the millions of people living in extreme poverty in the world's poorest countries and thought it unfair that some people have so much and others so little. What do these thoughts have to do with socialism and what is socialism?

A LOOK AT SOCIALISM

Socialism is a political and economic system with the key aim of making society more equal. However, supporters of socialism do not always agree about the best ways of achieving this ideal goal. There are different socialist "schools of thought" about how best to achieve a fair society. Some people oppose socialism. Many people in western societies support capitalism and do not agree with socialism. Opponents of socialism claim that socialist societies are just as unfair as capitalist societies, such as the United States, but simply in different ways.

Socialists believe that workers need to join together to gain more power in society.

UNDERSTANDING BETTER

GOVERNMENT SERVICES

Socialists usually believe that society will be fairer if more aspects of it are controlled by the state, or government. Can you think of ways in which you benefit from services that come from the government? Do you attend a public school? If so, it is provided by the state and is it paid for by taxes that the government collects from people in society. Some governments provide other services, such as maintaining highways, policing, and housing. Do you think governments should provide more or fewer services?

SOCIALIST IDEAS IN ACTION

Socialist ideas are present in many governments around the world today. Socialism is an influence when governments provide a welfare system or free medical care. It can help the poorer people in society by improving education, housing, and creating job opportunities. In some countries, socialism, and its extreme form communism, result in societies that severely restrict the freedom and actions of individual citizens. Force is used to make people follow socialism.

These socialist protestors are campaigning for greater equality in society.

The History of Socialism

Socialist ideas first started to appeal to large numbers of people during the Industrial Revolution. This was a time of enormous change, in which inventions in machinery changed the way people worked forever. The Industrial Revolution swept across Europe and North America from the late 1700s onward. However, the roots of socialism were probably laid long before that. The vision of socialism comes from the time when ancient thinkers turned their attention to dreaming up the ideal society.

THE FIRST SOCIALISTS

The earliest socialist ideas can be traced back to the ancient Greek thinker, Plato, who lived almost 2,500 years ago. Plato wrote *The Republic*, in which he imagined an ideal society. In this society people shared their property. This shared ownership was also a feature of early Christian communities, such as monasteries.

Plato's ideas about politics, philosophy, and many other subjects have had a profound influence on later thinkers in modern society.

EXPANDING CITIES

By the late 1800s, societies in Europe and North America were starting to change. Steam power was being used in large factories that employed hundreds of people. To work in the factories, people moved to live in huge, fast-growing cities. The American and French Revolutions of the late 1700s spread the idea that "all men are created equal," but the ideal did not usually include women and slaves. These ideas laid the foundations for the development of socialism.

One of the earliest socialists was Robert Owen. He was a successful industrialist who started a socialist community at New Harmony, Indiana.

A PERFECT SOCIETY

Over the centuries, socialist ideas appeared occasionally in writings about perfect societies. Small groups formed socialist communes, such as the Diggers in England, around 1650. The Diggers believed that land owned by the king and nobles, who had been defeated in the English Civil War, should be given to the poor so they could grow food. The Diggers faced resistance from government and local landowners who also wanted to claim the common land.

UNDERSTANDING BETTER

CHANGING SOCIETY

The early socialists, such as the Diggers, lived in small communities. By the 1800s, when socialist ideas began to gain popularity in new industrial cities, society was very different. Think about some of the changes that were taking place to understand why this happened:

People moved to live in cities.

The types of work people did changed rapidly.

It was easier for people to meet and share ideas.

7

Industrial Society

Building and running the factories and mills of the Industrial Revolution required lots of money, or capital. The businesspeople, who had capital to invest, became as rich as kings by selling the new manufactured goods that flowed from their factories. While these capitalists counted their money, the men, women, and often children who worked for them counted the cost. They worked very long hours in dangerous conditions for little money. Children as young as four spent up to ten hours a day working in factories or in mines, just to be able to earn enough money to survive.

WEALTH FOR ALL

The word "socialist" began to appear in the 1820s. Its meaning was the opposite of the word "capitalist," which meant great profit made by one or a few individuals. In socialism, the ideal was that factories would be owned in common, or by society, rather than by a few capitalists. Wealth created by the factories would be distributed among the workers.

The urban factories of the Industrial Revolution were very different from the farming economies of previous centuries.

UNDERSTANDING BETTER

WORKING PEOPLE

"The proletariat [working class] have nothing to lose but their chains. They have a world to win. Working men of the world, unite."

These are the last words of *The Communist Manifesto*. The working people were not literally in chains, so what do you think the authors, Friedrich Engels and Karl Marx, meant? How do they suggest the working class can be successful?

MARX AND ENGELS

Karl Marx and Friedrich Engels were the most important figures in the development of socialism. In 1848, they published *The Communist Manifesto*, which included their ideas about how society was organized. To Marx and Engels, communism and socialism were the same thing. They believed that history was all about the struggle between the ruling class, who owned farms and factories, and the working class, who owned nothing. Marx believed that when workers realized this, they would rise up against the oppressive ruling class.

ПОЧТАМ

4 К

1818 · КАРЛ МАРКС · 1883

ПОЧТА СССР · 1983

This stamp from the Soviet Union celebrates the influence of Karl Marx on socialist ideas.

Revolution

In the later years of the 1800s, socialist political parties began to form in countries across Europe. These early socialists believed, like Karl Marx, that they would only be able to have a say in society by defeating the ruling classes. One of the most extreme of these revolutionary socialists was Vladimir Lenin, the leader of Russia's Bolshevik Party.

SEIZING POWER

Lenin's chance for revolution came in 1917. World War I had been raging across Europe, and elsewhere, for three years when the Russian people overthrew Tsar Nicholas II. A temporary government was put in place. However, food was in short supply, prices were rising, and the Russian people's wish for control of more land was not met. After a turbulent year of revolution, Lenin and his group of revolutionaries seized power. They promised the people of Russia land, and an end to both war and food shortages. Lenin was determined to turn Russia into the world's first communist country—the Soviet Union.

Lenin masterminded the establishment of communism in Russia, but was ruthless in crushing all opposition to him.

ICH BIN EINE TERRORISTIN

⚠ *This is a street art image of Rosa Luxemburg, who led an unsuccessful socialist uprising in Germany at the end of World War I.*

SOCIAL DEMOCRATS

While communism in Russia inspired many socialists, others were put off the ideal as Russia became a communist dictatorship, which terrorized many of its own people. After World War I, many countries had also given working people the vote so other socialist political parties focused their attention on gathering votes rather than planning revolution.

The tough economic conditions of the years after World War I enabled some socialist parties, such as the British Labour Party, to grow. However, socialism came under attack from fascist parties in many countries.

UNDERSTANDING BETTER

NO VOTES FOR WORKERS

In the 1800s, ordinary working people, who might vote for socialist political parties, could not vote in elections in most countries. The ruling class was unlikely to vote for socialist political parties that threatened to remove much of their power. How do you think the ruling classes felt about the spread of socialist ideas? What do you think happened when people, including women, were free to vote in the early twentieth century? Do you think life got better or worse for working people?

Socialism in Power

The United States and the United Kingdom became allies of the Soviet Union as they battled against Germany, Italy, and Japan in World War II. At the end of the war, Soviet-style communist regimes spread across Eastern Europe. Western nations were determined to stand against what they saw as the evils of communism. However, as millions of people recovered from war, socialist ideas and parties were accepted in many countries.

In the United States, Eugene Debs was the most successful socialist candidate in the presidential election of 1920. However, he won only a small share of the total vote.

THE WELFARE STATE

In Britain, the government of Winston Churchill, which had led Britain through the war, was replaced by the Labour Party and prime minister Clement Attlee. This socialist government took many areas of industry and business into public ownership, meaning that they were owned and run by the state. They also launched a National Health Service, paid for through taxes, which was free for all citizens. These acts showed socialists that the capitalist system could be changed by elected politicians rather than revolution.

SOCIALISM SPREADS

After World War II, socialist governments were elected in many countries including Sweden, Denmark, and France. Communist regimes continued to hold power in the Soviet Union and Eastern Europe. In 1949, Mao Zedong's communists took power in China. Other communist regimes followed, including the Cuban government led by Fidel Castro.

At the time of the Great Depression, many families, such as this mother and her children, lost their income. Families became homeless and hungry through extreme poverty.

UNDERSTANDING BETTER

THE GREAT DEPRESSION

In the years after 1939, the United States and much of the world was hit by the Great Depression. Many businesses failed and one-quarter of Americans could not find work. There were no welfare payments at the time, and millions of people could not afford to buy enough food to survive. President Franklin Roosevelt introduced the "New Deal" to provide more jobs for people. Many people believed this was a socialist act. Roosevelt's New Deal was the largest, most expensive government plan in the history of the United States. What do you think it meant for the country's people?

The Crisis of Socialism

By the 1970s, it seemed to many people that socialism was replacing capitalism in some countries. However, this was an illusion. Both social democracy, which had been a feature of many democratic countries, and the hardline communism of the Soviet Union were in crisis.

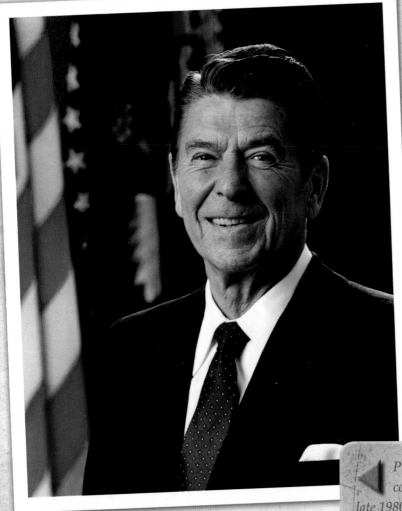

SOCIALISM COLLAPSES

In the late 1970s, critics of socialist ideas in western countries, such as the United States and Europe, grew louder. They argued that socialist measures, such as publicly owned businesses and free health care, were costly and inefficient. One of the most prominent supporters of this argument was US president Ronald Reagan, who held office from 1981 until 1989, and British prime minister Margaret Thatcher. The two politicans attracted votes from people who felt that welfare spending, and high taxes to pay for it, had stopped individuals from achieving success.

President Reagan believed that the collapse of communist governments in the late 1980s proved that socialism could not work.

TRIUMPH OF CAPITALISM

In 1989, the hated communist governments across Eastern Europe crumbled because of economic problems and people's wish to have the freedom they saw in western Europe and North America. The 28-mile-long (45-km-long) Berlin wall that split Germany in two, West and East, was finally breached in 1990. The two parts then merged to form a unified country. The Soviet Union broke up in 1991. Today, there are still communist or socialist governments in some countries, notably China, but many formerly socialist countries have adopted a capitalist system.

This graffiti is on the Berlin wall, which once divided communist East Berlin from the capitalist West Berlin.

UNDERSTANDING BETTER

WE ALSO DREAM

"Socialists ... can provide you shelter, fill your belly with bacon and beans, treat you when you're ill, all the things guaranteed to a prisoner or a slave. They don't understand that we also dream."

These words were spoken by Ronald Reagan and summed up his view on why capitalism would always be more successful than socialism. What did Reagan mean by saying that we also dream? What do we dream about that socialism can't provide?

CHAPTER TWO

Types of Socialism

The history of socialism shows that the political idea has many different strands and variations. Even in the early days of socialism, different thinkers developed their own socialist theories. As socialism has spread around the world and adapted to different cultures, it has also changed. Socialists today share many beliefs, but they disagree on many things, including how much they can compromise with capitalist society.

MODERN EXTREMES

We can see different types of socialism in different parts of the modern world. At one extreme is North Korea. This secretive state still clings to an extreme form of communism. This has brought its people extreme poverty and little food, while the country's resources are spent on its armed forces and the cult of its leaders. Food in the country is grown on collective farms. The government takes a large percentage of the food, leaving the rest for farmers.

At the other extreme, there is some evidence of socialist ideals in almost any country that provides its people with free education, welfare payments if they are out of work, or any state-funded health care insurance. Many people who would never call themselves socialist still believe that the state should provide state-funded programs to support citizens who need them.

Socialists disagree over whether individuals should own private property, and that does not just mean real estate.

For Sale

A Family Owned

Broker Company

MODERATE SOCIALISM

Between these two socialist extremes are countries that are governed by democratic socialist regimes, such as Brazil. The Workers' Party government of president Lula da Silva and his successor, Dilma Rousseff, has brought in state control of many industries to raise living standards for many of Brazil's poorest people.

UNDERSTANDING BETTER

SOCIALIST UTOPIA

Thomas More's *Utopia* describes an island on which land and houses were the common property of all the people. On the island, people swap houses every ten years so they do not envy each other's property. Money does not exist and people can take food and other goods they need from a general store. Do you think such a society could ever work? If not, what might stop it from working?

Thomas More published his ideas about an ideal, socialist society in 1516.

Democratic Socialism

The main focus of this book is democratic socialism, or social democracy. This is the form of socialism followed by mainstream socialist parties in democratic countries around the world. Social democracy grew from the same roots as more extreme revolutionary forms of socialism, but social democrats disagree strongly with the idea that socialism can be forced on a country through revolution.

GETTING ELECTED

Social democrats argue that democratic elections and processes are the best way to introduce socialist ideas. To win an election, socialist politicians have to explain how they will make life better for the people they want to vote for them. Through election campaigns, political candidates must win the votes of people in society by promising to provide the people with what they want.

Deciding which party to vote for is a very important decision in a democratic country.

MAKING A CHOICE

There are many questions people ask themselves when they're deciding who to vote for in an election. Some of these questions are:

Which party will make them richer? Socialist parties will normally ask wealthier people to pay more taxes, but they will provide more government services to those with less money.

Which government will provide the best schools, hospitals, and other services? Some people believe that these services are better if they are managed by the state. Others feel that private companies will serve customers more effectively in order to make bigger profits.

Which of the above issues and benefits are important to you and why?

GREATER CONTROL

Social democrats believe that the state should be more closely involved in people's lives, either by owning important businesses directly, or by making sure that they follow government rules. Social democrats pass laws to ensure that workers are treated fairly. This means that governments must spend more money, so they must ask people, particularly the wealthier members of society, to pay higher taxes. The next chapter explains how this type of socialism works.

If a socialist government charges higher taxes to pay for services, people may have less money to spend on themselves.

19

Revolutionary Socialism

Revolutionary socialists, or communists, are not concerned about getting elected. Like the first communist government in the Soviet Union, they take power by force rather than waiting to be elected. They follow the Marxist idea that society is a constant struggle between workers and the ruling or capitalist class.

COMMUNIST GOVERNMENTS

Communism is an extreme form of socialism in which most, or all, property in a country is owned by its government. People who live in communist countries do not normally have any choice about who governs them.

Most communist governments around the world took power many years ago, often with the support of the Soviet Union. Some countries, like China, have allowed private businesses to embrace capitalism. A few Chinese citizens have become wealthy. Socialists would argue that these citizens are not socialist at all.

UPRISING IN CZECHOSLOVAKIA

In 1948, in Czechoslovakia, communists supported by the Soviet Union carried out a coup. Leading politicians who supported democracy were arrested and imprisoned, and the communists then infiltrated the government. Shortly after, the Czech president was forced from power and replaced by the leader of the Czech communist party. In the late 1980s peaceful protests in the country resulted in the communist government giving up power and, elections were held in 1990. Soon afterward, the country split into two independent countries, Slovakia and the Czech Republic.

China's economy is changing, but the government still keeps tight control over the country and its people.

CASTRO'S CUBA

Cuba is one of the last communist regimes. Fidel Castro took power in Cuba after a revolution in 1959. Castro introduced communism to Cuba, and took total control of the country. Castro argued that by taking control of the country he improved education and health care for most Cubans. During the Cold War, Cuba was closely allied with the Soviet Union, a great threat to the United States at the time. As a result, Cuba still faces sanctions from the United States. In 2008, Fidel Castro handed over power to his brother, Raul, who has reformed Cuba so it is easier for businesses to operate there.

UNDERSTANDING BETTER

SOCIAL DEMOCRACY VS COMMUNISM

Looking at the examples on this page and the previous one, what are the main differences between social democracy and communism? Consider how communist governments take power, and how they treat their people when forming your answer.

North Korea has been ruled by a family of communist dictators since 1948. Although it claims to be "democratic," the country's people have no say in politics and many live in extreme poverty.

Other Forms of Socialism

Social democracy and communism have been the most common branches of socialism, but socialist ideas have often been adapted by other groups to suit their own campaigns. These groups include Christians, who felt that capitalist society went against Christian teaching by encouraging women to campaign for the right to vote.

NO STATE CONTROL

Anarcho-socialists are opposed to all forms of state control. They believe that without the control of the state, people will naturally cooperate with each other. This idea has never been tested in a whole country, but has been trialed by small groups. Anarcho-socialism was a feature of some small socialist groups, or communes, in the 1960s. It has also been used to justify terrorist acts against the state, such as those carried out by Red Brigades in Italy during the 1970s. The Red Brigades carried out more than 50 attacks against the state, including murders and kidnappings. The aim was to weaken and overthrow the Italian government and set up a revolutionary society run by the lower social classes.

Mikhail Bakunin was the founder of anarcho-socialism. He fought against capitalism, government, and religion.

DON'T TRUST THE STATE

Syndicalists had a similar distrust of the state. They were an extreme wing of the trade union movement, who were particularly active in the early 1900s. In trade unions, workers come together to argue for better pay and working conditions. Syndicalists believed that, through direct action and general strikes across many industries, they could destroy the government so workers could control their own factories.

UNDERSTANDING BETTER

WOMEN'S RIGHTS

In most countries, men were able to vote in elections long before women. Campaigners for women's voting rights often supported socialist ideas. Can you think of reasons why socialists might have helped the cause of campaigners for women's rights?

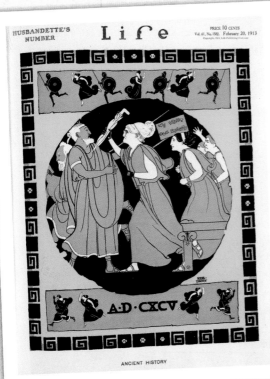

Susan B. Anthony (right and above) campaigned for women's voting rights in the United States. She was also a supporter of socialism, as were many campaigners for women's equality.

23

CHAPTER THREE

How Socialism Works

What is it like to live in a country run on socialist principles? Although all socialist political parties have slightly different ideas about how to put socialist ideas into practice, they do share certain beliefs about how to make countries fairer.

Some socialists are prepared to accept compromise with capitalism. This has been particularly true since the collapse of communist regimes and the decline of socialism in the 1980s and 1990s.

Sweden's wealthier people had to pay up to four-fifths of everything they earned in taxes to pay for the country's socialist policies during the 1980s.

SWEDISH SOCIALISM

Sweden is a country of 8 million people in northern Europe. Sweden had a socialist government for much of the twentieth century and is a good example of the principles of socialism in action. A socialist leader in the 1930s described Sweden as "a good home" which "does not consider anyone as privileged or underappreciated."

A FAIR SYSTEM

This idea of fairness was put into practice as Sweden devoted a high proportion of the country's wealth to providing health and education systems that would reduce inequality between people. The socialist party was extremely popular for many years, but was helped by strong trade unions that supported the rights of workers. Although the Swedish government did not take over businesses like other socialist countries, it worked with industry to ensure that workers were well treated, and had a say in how the businesses they worked in were run.

SOCIALIST STILL?

Like many countries that once embraced socialism, Sweden has changed. However, it still keeps many of its socialist policies in place. The rest of this chapter looks, in more detail, at different socialist policies.

Socialist regimes try to provide jobs for everyone. If people are unable to find work, social welfare provides money for food and other essentials.

UNDERSTANDING BETTER

TAX BENEFITS?

The people in Sweden are among the highest tax payers in the world. Why do you think the Swedish people are happy to hand over so much of what they earn in taxes to the government? What do they expect to get in return?

Public Ownership

The concern that workers were being exploited in factories, and other businesses, was one of the main reasons for the spread of socialist ideas. Public ownership of industries has been a central feature of many socialist governments.

Working in coal mines is hard work and can be very dangerous. Socialist governments often nationalize the coal-mining industry to protect workers' rights.

BETTER WORKING CONDITIONS

During the Industrial Revolution, workers lacked many of the things that employees today expect. There were no laws to stop children working in dangerous jobs, and there were no benefits, such as limited working hours and paid vacation. Most socialists felt that the only way to achieve better conditions was for workers to limit the power of private owners.

Socialist governments control private ownership by taking industries into public ownership, or nationalizing them. Nationalized industries are managed in the interest of the workers and the state. When they make profits, this money goes to the government to help fund public services that benefit the whole country. The workers benefit because they are paid a good salary, are entitled to paid vacation, and receive sick pay.

FAIRER BUT LESS EFFICIENT?

However, when things go badly for nationalized industries, the cost of this has to then be covered by the government. Where private businesses might reduce their costs by employing fewer people, businesses in public ownership are under pressure to look after their workers. Critics of socialism argue that this makes them very inefficient. They argue that a business run mainly to benefit its workers will not be able to respond to changing conditions.

Bill Gates became one of the world's richest men by founding the company Microsoft, which created jobs for thousands of people. Could this have happened under socialism?

UNDERSTANDING BETTER

FREE ENTERPRISE

In the United States, most businesses are owned and managed by private individuals, although there may be strict regulations from government about how they can do business. Workers in this type of business may have lower pay or fewer vacations than those in nationalized businesses elsewhere. However, private businesses are often more successful than state-owned ones. Which system do you think is better for workers? Which one is better for customers?

Central Planning

Socialists argue that without government control, most ordinary people's opportunities in life will be damaged by the actions of a few wealthy or powerful people. For this reason, socialist governments are involved in many areas of people's lives.

To help manage the lives of its citizens, socialist governments often employ more officials, called bureaucrats, than capitalist governments.

TARGETS AND WAGES

In countries where most businesses are owned and run by the government, each industry may have targets for how much money it makes, and how workers are paid and treated. In nonsocialist countries, there may also be general targets, or rules, about how workers should be paid that cover all industries. For example, many countries have a minimum wage that all workers should be paid. This is likely to be higher under a socialist government.

An entrepreneur is anyone who comes up with ideas to make money. Opponents argue that socialism stops people from becoming entrepreneurs.

DOES CENTRAL PLANNING WORK?

Critics of socialism argue that socialist "big government" actually makes a country less successful. By telling people how to live their lives, socialists stop them from acting on their own individual initiative. If people are allowed to act on their own, they come up with new ideas that create wealth and jobs. Huge governments are not good at coming up with these kinds of new ideas and, therefore, individuals may be held back under a socialist government.

UNDERSTANDING BETTER

BETTER PAY MEANS BETTER RESULTS

"The commonest laborer who sweeps the floor shall receive his $5 per day. We believe in making 20,000 men prosperous and contented rather than … making a few slave drivers in our establishment millionaires." Henry Ford.

Henry Ford is not usually known as a socialist but he decided to pay his workers twice as much as other carmakers, and it worked. His workers were happy to work and, therefore, worked harder and faster, resulting in the production of more cars. The price of the cars dropped, which meant that the workers could also afford to buy the vehicles themselves. Why do you think Henry Ford decided to pay his workers more money?

Public Services

We take for granted that all young people in western countries will have the opportunity to go to school until their late teenage years, without having to pay for it. This was not always the case, and still does not happen in many poorer parts of the world.

▼ Despite the spread of public services, many of the world's people still live without basic health care.

EDUCATION FOR EQUALITY

Elementary schooling for all children was actually introduced around the time socialist ideas were being developed. Since then, levels of education have continued to rise, even in countries such as the United States, where socialists have not held power. Socialists see public education as a way to increase equality in society. If people are educated equally, they are equally able to get good jobs or start businesses, and therefore obtain a more equal standard of living.

INTRODUCING HEALTH CARE

The communist government of the Soviet Union introduced free health care for all citizens, soon after the Russian Revolution. This was followed by other public health care systems, particularly in the years after World War II, when the British National Health Service was created. Other countries, such as the United States and Canada, provide free health care to certain groups, such as the elderly. In developed countries where there is no free health care for younger citizens, most people have to buy medical insurance.

Prior to 1960, Cuba had a poor record on health care and education. Giving people full access to these services has led to great improvements, in spite of the country's many other problems. However, the vast cost of providing free public services for everyone is causing many countries to cut back on the services they provide.

In many developing countries, governments cannot raise enough money to provide health and welfare services. Medical care is instead provided by charities and nongovernmental organizations.

UNDERSTANDING BETTER

WHO PAYS FOR PUBLIC SERVICES?

When socialist governments promise to spend more on health, education, and welfare, whose money are they spending? They are spending money collected from the people through taxes. In a socialist system, taxes are likely to be much higher for wealthy people than they are for poorer people. In effect, richer people pay more for these services. Do you think it is fair that the higher-earning people in society pay more for public services than those people who earn less?

Power for Workers

The early socialists wanted to replace capitalism with a more equal society, in which power would be handed over to the workers. While communist regimes in many countries achieved this goal, many socialists were appalled by the lack of freedom under these regimes. Instead, social democrats tried to change capitalism to meet the needs of workers, rather than replacing it entirely.

POWER IN A UNION

Trade unions had an important role in limiting the power of capitalism and were often directly linked to socialist political parties. On their own, workers have little power as they can lose their jobs if they complain about pay and conditions. However, if workers come together and unite they have more power because there are more of them. For example, if workers are not happy about an issue, such as pay or conditions, they can stop work and strike to get what they want.

Trade unions have had a big influence in shaping the rights that workers in many industries now enjoy, such as paid vacations and a limit to the number of hours that employees have to work each week.

Trade union history has seen many battles between socialist unions, their employers, and governments to win more workers' rights.

EQUAL RIGHTS FOR WOMEN

In the past, trade unions were often hostile to women workers, who might take men's jobs or work for lower wages. In recent decades, many more women have worked outside the home. Many feminist groups have used socialist arguments in their attempts to win equal working rights.

> *Women in many countries have been able to work because of social welfare measures, such as free childcare or education.*

UNDERSTANDING BETTER

UNDER PRESSURE

In recent decades, the power of trade unions has lessened in many areas. There are several reasons why this has happened:

- Industries in many developed countries have changed. Fewer people are working in big factories and heavy industries.

- Many businesses are more global, so work can be moved overseas.

- Politicians have passed new laws to limit the power of unions.

Can you think of other reasons why unions are less powerful? Look at news sources to find industries and countries where unions are still strong.

CHAPTER FOUR

Living with Socialism

It is clear that socialism has had an impact on many countries, even those without a socialist government or popular socialist party. Socialist measures, such as free health care, can help to safeguard members of society who cannot afford health insurance. What is it like to live in a country with a socialist government?

SOCIALISM IN VENEZUELA

Hugo Chavez promised an end to poverty and corruption when he was elected as president of Venezuela in 1998. When he died in 2013, he was mourned by millions of Venezuelans, although he had as many enemies as friends. Chavez was elected, but made sure that he filled important jobs within his government with his friends, to ensure loyalty. He also broke the rules when he needed to hold on to power.

In 2006, Chavez introduced what he called "twenty-first century socialism" in Venezuela. The socialist leader had previously announced "missions" to make health care and adult education available to Venezuela's poor. His successes included reducing Venezuela's level of unemployment, cutting the number of people living in extreme poverty, and improving health care so fewer Venezuelans died in childhood.

Hugo Chavez improved the lives of many Venezuelans through his socialist policies. As a result, the country showed an outpouring of grief over his death.

UNDERSTANDING BETTER

SOUTH AMERICAN SOCIALISM

South America is one part of the world where socialist parties have had success in recent years. Chavez formed alliances with socialist governments in Bolivia and Ecuador. Brazil, the largest country in the region, has also elected socialist governments. South American countries have often faced big social inequalities. Many countries have a few very rich people but extreme poverty for much of the population. Why do you think people have elected socialist governments in these countries?

GOOD AND BAD

Chavez's successes were made a lot easier by Venezuela's oil wealth. Exports of oil more than quadrupled between 1999 and 2011. Chavez also nationalized many of the country's main industries during his time in power. However, the country also paid a heavy price for his leadership. Corruption within the country continued and Chavez ruled largely by personal power. He was also an outspoken critic of the United States.

Drawbacks of Socialism

Hugo Chavez's regime in Venezuela is an example of a socialist system that achieved good, but was flawed in many ways. There are similar examples in recent history. Many extreme socialist or communist governments have been a disaster for the people they claimed to help. In the 1970s and 1980s, the Vietnamese faced famine after their communist government made the transportation of food and goods between provinces illegal, and took control of businesses and farms. Many people were forced to work on the land and thousands were executed for trying to flee the country.

Red Square in Moscow was the center of the communist world before the end of the Soviet Union in 1991.

RIGHTS, FREEDOMS, AND RESTRICTIONS

Extreme socialist regimes usually arise from revolution and war, such as the government of the Soviet Union after 1917 and Fidel Castro's Cuba after 1959. While they may have achieved success in some areas, such as improving education, there have been major drawbacks. Central planning and nationalization of industries may have created more equality, but people have often faced poverty. Communist states, from East Germany to North Korea, have also restricted the freedom and human rights of their people.

UNDERSTANDING BETTER

IS CAPITALISM PERFECT?

As well as questioning whether socialism can ever be successful, we should also ask the same questions about capitalism. Can a system that allows huge inequality between rich and poor really be the best option?

SOCIALISM DOESN'T WORK?

Even democratic socialism faces criticism. Supporters of pure capitalism argue that humans are naturally competitive and selfish. We will always try to beat the system or gain power over others. The idea that all people will cooperate in a socialist society is doomed to fail.

Countries that practice socialism may provide benefits and security for their people, but this normally involves the loss of some personal freedom (even if it is just the freedom to get rich). Capitalists also argue that giving extra rights to workers will eventually lead to job losses, because of competition from other countries.

Many Cubans still drive cars and live in buildings that have hardly changed in decades. People argue that Cuba failed to modernize when the socialist government took power in 1959.

Opposing Socialism

In the decades after World War II, the United States, and other capitalist countries, were concerned that the Soviet Union wanted to spread communism and socialism across the world. The United States, and its allies, opposed the Soviet Union in a political struggle known as the Cold War. During this time, many countries in the West elected socialist governments.

Extreme socialist regimes, from Russia to Venezuela, often restrict the freedom of newspapers and other media to criticize the government.

CONTROLLING THE PEOPLE

Socialist governments that sprang up after World War II were often oppressive. The socialist governments in Eastern Europe did everything they could to prevent protests by their own people, including the use of secret police and military force. In 1980, Polish workers formed an independent trade union, called Solidarity, and went on strike at a shipyard in the city of Gdansk. They wanted better working conditions and more political freedom. Strikes broke out across Poland and sowed the seeds for the end of communism in Poland. Solidarity leader, Lech Walesa, became the first freely elected president of Poland in 1990.

Those who oppose socialism strongly are often the people who benefit most from capitalism, such as business leaders. However, many less wealthy people also believe that government should not interfere in people's lives. Less interference means lower taxes—and more money for individuals to spend.

SOCIALISM IN THE UNITED STATES

"Socialism never took root in America because the poor see themselves not as an oppressed proletariat but as temporarily embarrassed millionaires."

American writer John Steinbeck was trying to answer the question why socialism has never become a big political force in the United States. His suggestion was that Americans believed they could all become rich and did not accept the idea of a struggle between the working class and capitalism. Although the United States has never been run under a socialist government, what areas of socialism has the country embraced?

The American Tea Party movement campaigns for lower taxes and against paying for public services.

CHAPTER FIVE

A Future for Socialism?

Socialism faced its greatest crisis in the 1990s, after the collapse of communist governments in Eastern Europe and the Soviet Union. Some governments still claimed to be socialist or communist, such as in China. However, most economies started to move toward a capitalist system. Is socialism an idea that has had its day, or does it have a future?

A THIRD WAY

In developed countries, such as those in western Europe, socialist parties have adapted. Many leading politicians have argued that equality and welfare are just as important to people as they always had been, but socialist ideas about workers controlling factories cannot deliver a sustainable system of government. Instead, politicians have proposed a "third way" of governing fairly, but without socialism. Leaders who have argued for this "third way" include former US president Bill Clinton and former British prime minister Tony Blair.

Newly prosperous young people in fast-growing nations, such as China, are more likely to see the benefits of capitalism.

DEVELOPING COUNTRIES

Beyond the western world, the story has been different. In developing countries, where many people live in poverty, heavy industry has increased. Many people are now employed in industry, but still live in poverty with very few workplace rights. In countries such as Brazil and Venezuela, where workers often have few rights, socialist governments have taken power. It is likely that countries such as these will remain socialistic in the near future.

This ruined office building in Detroit, Michigan, is a reminder that many jobs in traditional industrial cities have moved to developing countries.

UNDERSTANDING BETTER

THE CHANGING WORLD OF WORK

The way people work has changed. The mines and factories in Europe and North America, where socialist ideas took hold, have closed down or moved overseas. People are now more likely to work in call centers or huge grocery stores. Most workers in developed countries are no longer part of a trade union. How do these changes affect socialist ideas? Are people still interested in issues such as equality and having a say in their workplace?

Crisis for Capitalism?

As communist regimes collapsed in many parts of the world in the 1990s, it seemed as if capitalism had beaten socialism. However, in the years after 2008, capitalism faced a crisis that caused some people to question the system itself. The crisis started when people discovered that banks had taken huge risks in lending money to people who could not repay it. This included lending to people to buy houses that they couldn't afford. The banking system is so complex that many of these risks had been passed on to other banks all over the world—without the banks being aware of this.

THE SECOND GREAT RECESSION

Governments in the United States, Europe, and elsewhere had to give the banks billions of dollars to make up for their catastrophic losses. People were angry when they saw the enormous sums of money they had paid in taxes being given to high-earning bankers. Some banks were even nationalized in some countries in a bid to resolve the problem.

People in Greece were particularly badly affected by the 2008 economic crisis. Capitalists and socialists were both blamed for causing the country's problems.

A RETURN TO SOCIALISM?

The banking crisis caused such huge problems in the world economy that many people lost their jobs and their homes. People expressed their anger in mass demonstrations that criticized the capitalist system.

Will this crisis see growing support for socialist parties? While some claim the 2008 recession proved the flaws in capitalism, many governments reacted by cutting spending on social welfare, and other services, in an attempt to reduce their countries' debts. Today, in most countries, the idea of a socialist state seems further away than ever.

UNDERSTANDING BETTER

WEALTH INEQUALITY

The richest 1 percent of Americans own more than one-third of all the country's wealth. More than four-fifths of the wealth is owned by the richest one-fifth of Americans. This inequality increased after 2008, as poorer people were hit harder by the recession that began in that year. Do you think inequality is a bad thing? What do you think could be done to reduce it?

US president Barack Obama had to pour government money into businesses, including banks and car companies, as capitalism faced one of its greatest crises in 2008.

43

What Have You Learned?

In this book, we have learned that socialism comes in many forms, but all socialists share some common beliefs. We know that socialist ideas have existed since ancient times. However, the detailed theories of socialism developed fully during the Industrial Revolution, particularly in the socialist writings of Karl Marx and Friedrich Engels.

UNDERSTANDING SOCIALISM

We have discovered the different ways that revolutionary socialists and social democrats seek to gain power, and the key differences between socialism and capitalism. We know about socialist ideas such as public ownership of industries and central planning, and the benefits and drawbacks of these ideas. We have also discovered how people have opposed socialist ideas.

Anticapitalist protestors camped out on many streets to demonstrate against the capitalist corruption they believed caused the 2008 financial crisis and recession.

A RENEWED INTEREST

The years since the early 1990s have been difficult ones for socialism around the world, as socialist governments have changed and adapted. The example of socialist governments in South America, and the experience of the 2008 recession in developed countries, may lead to renewed interest in socialism as a way of organizing society.

UNDERSTANDING BETTER

WHAT NOW?

Using what you have learned about socialism, study some of the socialist governments around the world to find out how they operate. Look at both elected socialist governments and socialist dictatorships, such as Cuba and North Korea. How do they treat their people and do they provide services such as health care? How do these countries differ from your own?

After the shock of the 2008 recession, socialists are adapting to a rapidly changing world.

SOCIALISM

GLOSSARY

ally a country that supports another one because of an agreement or treaty, such as in a war

bureaucrat a government official

capital money that is invested in something

capitalist an economic system that depends on people investing money to make and sell products. Someone with money to invest is a capitalist

citizen a member of a country

Cold War the state of hostility that existed between the United States, Soviet Union, and their allies, between 1945 and 1990

communist a person or political party that believes all property should be controlled by the government, with everyone working for the state

corruption making illegal payments to public officials, or others, in exchange for receiving special treatment

democracy a system in which the government is voted for by most, or all, of the adults in that country

developed country a country in which industry and the economy are fully formed, such as the United States

developing country a country in which industry and the economy are still forming. Average wealth of people in developing countries is usually less than that of people in developed countries.

dictatorship rule by an unelected person, or group, who have seized power, for example, after a revolution

entrepreneur a person who starts a business to make a profit

equality having the same rights and opportunities as other people

fascist a strongly nationalist or extreme right-wing political party or government

feminist believing in equal rights for women

human rights rights that every human being has, regardless of where they live

independence standing on its own. When a country is independent it has its own government

Industrial Revolution major change and development of manufacturing and heavy industry in a country, as happened in many countries after the British Industrial Revolution of the late 1700s

industrialist a person who owns a factory or large industrial business

manufactured anything that is made by people from raw materials, such as goods made in a factory

political party a group of people with similar ideas about how a country should be run

propaganda the spreading of information to influence public opinion or present the person creating the information in a favorable way

public ownership when industries or businesses are owned by the government and operated for the benefit of all people in a country

revolution a violent upheaval to overthrow a ruler or bring radical change

sanctions trade or other restrictions imposed on a country by the international community in order to force its government to change their policy

secret police security officers who maintain security within a country, particularly in secretive or repressive governments

Soviet Union a union of countries in Eastern Europe, led by Russia, which lasted until 1991

trade union organization made up of all workers in a business or industry, to give them more bargaining power with employers than they would have individually

FOR MORE INFORMATION

BOOKS

Donovan, Sandy and Caryn Gracey Jones. *Teens in Venezuela*. North Mankota, MN: Compass Point, 2007.

Jarnow, Jessie. *Socialism: A Primary Source Analysis*. New York, NY: Rosen, 2004.

Newman, Michael. *Socialism: A Very Short Introduction*. Oxford, UK: Oxford University Press, 2005.

Rees, Fran. *Fidel Castro: Leader of Communist Cuba*. North Mankota, MN: Compass Point, 2006.

WEBSITES

Discover more about the story of socialism at:
u-s-history.com/pages/h1669.html

Find out about socialism and economy at:
money.howstuffworks.com/socialism1.htm

Discover more about socialism around the world at:
worldsocialism.org/index.php

INDEX

American Revolution 7
anarcho-socialists 22
Anthony, Susan B. 23

Bakunin, Mikhail 22
Berlin wall 15
Bolshevik Party 10
Brazil 17, 35, 41
Britain 7, 11, 12, 14, 31, 40

capitalism 4, 8, 12, 14, 15,
    20, 22, 24, 32, 37, 38, 39,
    40, 42–43, 44
Castro, Fidel 13, 21, 36
Chavez, Hugo 34–35, 36
China 13, 15, 20, 40
Clinton, Bill 40
Cold War 21, 38
communism 5, 9, 10–11, 12,
    13, 14, 15, 16, 20–21, 22,
    24, 31, 32, 36, 38, 40
Cuba 13, 21, 31, 36, 37, 45
Czechoslovakia 20

Debs, Eugene 12
decline of socialism 14–15,
    24, 40
democratic socialism 14, 17,
    18–19, 37
Denmark 13

Eastern Europe 12, 13, 15,
    38, 40
education 5, 16, 21, 25,
    30–31, 33, 34, 36
elections 12, 18, 19, 20, 23,
    38
Engels, Friedrich 9, 44

fascism 11
feminists 33
Ford, Henry 29
France 7, 13
French Revolution 7

Gates, Bill 27
global financial crisis 35,
    42–43
Great Depression 13
Greece 42

health care 12, 14, 16, 21,
    25, 30, 31, 34, 45
history of socialism 6–15,
    16

Industrial Revolution 6, 8,
    26, 44

Labour Party (UK) 11, 12
Lenin, Vladimir 10
Luxemburg, Rosa 11

Marx, Karl 9, 10
More, Thomas 17

nationalized industries
    26–27, 35, 36, 42
New Deal 13
North Korea 16, 21, 36, 45

Obama, Barack 43
Owen, Robert 7

Plato 6
Poland 38
private property 16
public services 5, 12, 16, 19,
    26, 30–31, 39, 43

Reagan, Ronald 14, 15
revolutionary socialism 6,
    7, 10–11, 20–21
Roosevelt, Franklin D. 13
Russia/Soviet Union 9,
    10–11, 13, 14, 15, 20, 21,
    31, 36, 38, 40

socialist governments
    12–13, 15, 26–27, 28, 31,
    34–37, 38, 41, 45
South America 17, 34–35,
    41, 45
state control 5, 17, 22,
    28–29, 36, 38
Sweden 13, 24–25

taxes 5, 12, 14, 19, 25, 31, 38,
    39, 42
Thatcher, Margaret 14
trade unions 23, 25, 32, 33,
    38

United States 4, 7, 12, 13,
    14, 21, 23, 27, 30, 31, 35,
    38, 39, 40, 41, 42, 43

Venezuela 34–35, 36, 38, 41
Vietnam 36
voting 11, 18, 19, 22, 23

wealth inequality 35, 37, 43
women's rights 22, 23, 33
workers 7, 8, 9, 11, 17, 19,
    20, 23, 25, 26, 27, 28, 29,
    32–33, 37, 38, 40, 41
World War I 10, 11
World War II 12, 13, 31, 38

Zedong, Mao 13, 20, 44